CADDISH

Also by Susana Gardner

HERSO An Heirship in Waves (Black Radish Books, 2011)
(lapsed insel weary) (The Tangent, 2008)

CADDISH

SUSANA GARDNER

Copyright 2013

www.blackradishbooks.org

Grateful acknowledgement is made to the editors of the following publications in which poems from this book have appeared: *Blart,* ed. Stephen Emmerson; *Boog City Reader,* guest ed. Buck Downs, *Cannibal,* eds. Katy Henriksen and Matthew Henriksen; *Knives Forks and Spoons Press (UK) 18's Anthology,* ed. Mark Cobley; *Capitalism Nature Socialism,* ed. Jules Boykoff; *Coupremine,* ed. Erik Rezpka, *Turntable and Blue Lights,* ed. Arielle Guy; *The Volta,* ed. Kate Greenstreet; and *VLAK2,* eds. Louis Armand, and David Vichnar; as well as to the collective publishing endeavours of *Delirious Hem, Black Radish Books* and *Dusie.* The cover image was first published as a vispo image in *Summerstock Literary Journal,* eds. Tim Armentrout, Joseph Cooper, Elizabeth Guthrie, Jared Hayes and Andrew K. Peterson.

Cover design and book design by Susana Gardner and Black Radish Books
Cover Image: *BEAUTY,* Susana Gardner

First printing, 2013 in the United States of America.

All rights reserved. No part of this book may be reproduced without the publisher's written permission, except for brief quotations in reviews.

ISBN: 978-0-9850837-7-9
ISSN: 2013932876

BLACK RADISH BOOKS, USA

CONTENTS

9   *Artless Adores Her*

13   *Idylls & Rushes*

35   *Because the Shell Half-Swallowed Her*

49   *Cuntstruck Lithe Guttersnipes*

81   *CADDISH*

99   *Triumph of Love*

LOVE the hideous in order to find the sublime core of it.
from Aphorisms on Futurism — Mina Loy

Artless Adores Her

Artless
    Adores her itinerant
Quivering Sea of voices

Painted
    Image   legible
Iridescent rich& lush

Binding December   alone
    Eat your early paradox:
Dirty Cloak Industry

Artless is
    Radiant exultant
Contractions of little mugs

Heaving& rising
    Incident me:
Come, Come, Come!

Answer mechanically
    Thoughts persist
Alcohol tedious   thereafter

Inward damp imbecilic
    Dress   half undone
Evident atrocity

Ought I leave?
    His harlot artfulness
Wanton carmine-tinted menacing

Ardent
    Wakefulness desiring
Luscious lips   diminish

Half-ships
    Idempotent   perfidy
Apogeic maxims

Idylls & Rushes

*To write is the joy and the torment of the idle.
Oh to write!*

Sidonie-Gabrielle Colette

(one)

Alone in that cage
her idle hands   interlace
garden-phlox   embellished
shapes color copy
her   otherwise she

(one)

Lucid hem   what face
fishes me out   dressing-room
my master-chance. I
feel over-sure in his
unruly kingdom.

(one)

Whimsical-bounty me
      (on the hem of her frock)
spirit my high-flimsy till dawn
slightly drunk   threading years.

(one)

Freedom others bitter tonic
subtle certainties proof reflection
idiosyncratic looking-glass woman
among nuances class
rhythmical language, thought.

(one)

Hypnotized idyll orgies
Or—the page, stage-right:
fever frantic rebels
            Oh, cheap carnations
overture less
ladyscape, light.

(one)

Fate, keep away   conquest
bouquet deference   silent their
letters—physical, urgent,
brutal.   Awkward
my garrulous love, idylls& rushes.

(one)

Your dark ugly mug, my new
darling self-abandonment!
At dawn, leafing wrack &ruin
piecing the scene original.

(one)

Unchartered old-fashioned gooseflesh
time married   again&
again bartering off my sounds
living off my gestures like garnishes.

(one)

Delicate fêted idyll—exculpated
faults—risk utter ruin first—
false common-place friends, do-gooders
imprisoned ego moneyed towers.

(one)

Isolation?   Yes.   Obstinate
rebuffing of   vile public   want
while daylight bounds after me in
rushes   dry scattered leaves.

(one)

In spite of myself,   I hear
the fusses and idylls. The *hush-
hush*   static in my ears,
the droning.

(one)

I rush against the tarnished
sun's wild tempering   off
any irksome mental fizzle
I arrive honey-combed
well-done-up.

(one)

I've heard your bull-dog bitch.
Winter coughs her up like the
women hastening buzzard's shit
about your neck.

(one)

Kind-hearted carcasses of matter:
an audience! Feed them your public
want, indigent scraps pander your
$15 post-modern fare.

(one)

Nothing is real   but   gesture
half-naked undulating concrete& volatile
gesture pouring forth rhythm and
new translation swaying &swaying.

(one)

Clear-sighted—on behalf of the
charmed toughs, I go—awkward
spurred imaginings—ardor,
admiration,   bowing in fusses.

Because the Shell Half-Swallowed Her

Because The Shell Half-Swallowed Her

       SEA
  SEA

Namesake driven, now divine.

Because The Shell Half-Swallowed Her
      She was left half-whole —
          Half-mollusk as it were
               and half-Her!

       SEA
  SEA

Half-her and half complicit — her legs!
IMMER running
running running
from the OTHER

Because the Shell Half-Swallowed Her
Her Porcelain Legs, O!
Her Lower Half!
Her awkward skirts!

       SEA
SEA

Her mouth amuck —Crustacean
Voice amniotic

Circuitous abalone
strands about her hair

Because the Shell Half-Swallowed Her
She is now half-there

She is NOW HALF THERE!
YES! She is now HOUSED there!

SEA
SEA

Because the Shell Half-Swallowed Her
Her Shoulders Cower So!
Her back bends alternately
in the arch of forever

O! ASTERN
Seahouse Encasement Subjective

SEA
SEA

Isolated anew.

Try her on for size!
All men do!

Snailed and spiraled blue her shell
her sea, her sea her NOW.

       SEA
SEA

>   But she may wreckon you!
>   Yes, she may wreckon you.
>
> LOVE!
> Oh?
>
> Love, you tried her on for size?
>
>
>   SEA
>   SEA

HMMMM! How silly this sounds to Her!
　　　　Her ear Aft—Abaft—Aback!

　　O, she hears your wild drone.
　　But Sea! forever harbours her

　　　　　　　　SEA
　　　SEA

Hell! Closest to the Sea now — E now!
She will tell you whatever you hope to hear.

What do you hope to hear?

                        SEA
        SEA

> Her hair a wild tangle,
> her note not of your range —
> Her Siren folds
> elongating — her
> treble beat precise
> sending you off now unrequited —
> Mainmast far-flung from her reach

          SEA
  SEA

O, Prodigious Son take care.

Because The Shell Half-Swallowed Her
THE SEA HALF-SWALLOWED HER!

And she will swallow you too.
She may have already swallowed you.

Yes, as she is there, she is through.

                SEA
SEA

*Cuntstruck
Lithe Guttersnipes*

Cuntstruck
Lithe Guttersnipes

<<A MANIED FEST>>

O, Nightcreatures, Come Out!

An urge so strong it is as if one has been cuntstruck.
Emily Critchley

Your nipples dragging through my totally cliched heart.
Cunt-ups, Dodi Bellamy

So throw off your stupid cloak
embrace all that you fear
For joy shall conquer all despair
in my Blakean year
My Blakean Year, Patti Smith

Cuntstruck Lithe Guttersnipes.
My terrible little tarts,
O, cheeky little know-it-alls!

[with whom I no longer claim to understand the
language of fiction]

My darling disagreeables,
My easily distractables —

Who dastardly streak sheer fastidiousness in shimmering tights...

Who stave off beauty & darkness
&run beside me on a lark.

Mien! Mien!

CUNTSTRUCK

My mewling pretty witty kitties—
Indeterminable as the Sun

Stroking SHE progressives—Strolling
around like Ladies of the Hour—

With Despondently wilted Lady Gaga Headdresses.

Festooned Whirling Bird dervishes—

Uterine—

CUNTSTRUCK

Wetting forget-me nots, poppycocks & starlings

Courting Russian Dandy Dalliances.

Let us tread assimilation laconic.

Let us give the Giant Mastiff something juicy to eat!

CUNTSTRUCK

Since we are all so damn precious and magnanimous.
Since we are all so damn complex&
we are all so damn damned&
DAMED.

Burrowing out of solitude in Kingston.
Borrowing the conductors sharpie —
with great parts of the day mere
flippant Imaginings —

CUNTSTRUCK

And so, the sound was never enough!
Delay doesn't hear her holler as
she stalls in triumphantly &all
out of breath into the room of halves—

CUNTSTRUCK

With our flippant moody brothers
in enormous hats who soon forget
to grasp at words with
words&so we stab at the air
at the concierge...
we junction ourselves
Beavering Inward—

CUNTSTRUCK

Among pyramid scheming &aversions
&yet, my lips feel nothing without Hope or
Courage &livery backwood cheekiness.

Bell-brained hours!

      Inward Cartography!

Pierce my inward momenture.

Among signage —

&Ocean
          &Ocean
                    &Ocean!

CUNTSTRUCK

Call me your devoted lithe Cuntkin
So Iconic.

ICONIC

Cunt Kinds be damned!

We dame the night — coupleted.
We complete the gauzy mechanical
Coitus Interruptus — in the moon-headed,
in the star-burnt night.

Ignited —

CUNTSTRUCK

To pitch her voice—stomach drawn in.
Bitch wants to dance.

To pitch his not once said "Bitch" under silks.

All red wide welcome home presentations.

I realize his greedy exasperation &call for Red Minutes,

Alone, alone, alone. *RI Inherness*. Yes!

Mixed in with chowder, narrow lanes & fishery charm.

She stalls Ocean Pastural—She frets boundless verse when she is told she should really

Consider short stories, for crying
Out loud—

CUNTSTRUCK

Were music enough it might have already happened.
Hear her wayward artisté!

Realize starlings were star-rings and that the stagecoach already left. That the sound is never enough and it will not sustain her&
she will
already search out the subsequent pitch& lay.

Yes. You, were never enough—

CUNTSTRUCK

The KING'S WORLD CLOCK knocks me on the head,
makes me weak in the knees,
beg for Repent& Repeat.

Beg for seconds...
all the while . . . *bitte, bitte, bitte* . . .

The KING makes me reassess BEAUTY — Tells Lies.

O — where every FEELING is
REIFIED, REEFED & RIFFED
Into the night — soon realized,
Abandoned —

CUNTSTRUCK

Concurrent SWEAT BREADS.

Concurrent SWEET BOXES.

The KING makes me reassess BEAUTY — Tell Lies.

    Oui.

Tells me not to ingest it.

    >>DO NOT INGEST IT!<<

Do not IN JEST me Sir,-!

...No, I shall not ingest it...

CUNTSTRUCK

I so want to prattle on!

    ACH!

bitte, bitte, bitte —

I want to rest in his ear, I want
the KING to feel me there...
and there...

    Oh, there!

CUNTSTRUCK

I want the KING to feel incredulous.
I want the KING to FEEL.

As I am Whip-smart
as I am Brave—the subject
of a portrait, even, if only for one moment.

One precise moment!

      I fixate on it—

CUNTSTRUCK

I feel better than even, even so, I
write this missive for when it is through.

For when you have left me, for
when I have left you.

I am hardly here now, even.
Where the Ocean is absent.

        ABSENT!

CUNTSTRUCK

AGOG.
 ARIGHT.

But, I try to make sense of it and feel
the failure in the very grasp at...attempt at...

Uncertainty.

But I still grasp.

As I have learned to embrace what I fear.

And you?

CUNTSTRUCK

If I could love, I would—
You—

Read the space like Duncan,
like a pro—there is only space here

For you—

CUNTSTRUCK

In this doggerel space
the KING hawks pages and

Itineraries—and reticent Starfucker vocabularies
Fuck-lists.

O, the KING is a big flirt and he knows it.

The KING names names is full on
Garden Subjectivity and proximates,
pantooning great Vestiges—

GREEDY FISHPAPER BEASTS!

O the KING is a Rockabilly Dodo bird—
a real gem—

CUNTSTRUCK

O

Morpheus!

Will you spread your arms about me?

O, Mr. Machine,

Will you translate my storied wave-length wave-verse minutes here?

O, will you wile me into your night...

Culling...   culling...

CUNTSTRUCK

As the Sea is a stave

       Splinter me

Dash me into your night!

O, Herren of Oft repeat of Mein Flammen-Tanz dreams

O, Smash me into bits!

Destroy me again and again.

Take me and the Inward rants home again, already—

CUNTSTRUCK

O GREEDY FISHPAPER CAMP. O Cuntstruck and Cocksure Heebygeeby Notion Camp! O False Friend Camp! O False Form Camp. O False Front Camp. Camp of the Cliché Careerist Camp Camp. O FALSE ADORATION CAMP! Camp of the Occupied — of the Oppressed &Oppressers Camp. Camp of the CAMP Camp. O Dreamy Sublime Camp for You. For you, who does not want to be loved Camp and for you, who ONLY wants to be loved Camp. This is for YOU, who does not know HOW to love Camp. O, Herr TRY IT ON for size camp! *O, Learn to Read the Damn Signs Camp.* O, for this Apolitical Void Camp. O, Opportunist Undisciplined Poetry Camp Camps. *O, Let's Make a New School or Movement Camp!* O, Weezleworded Manifesto Camp. O, Sir Light-to-the-Touch Camp! O, Master of Divergent Wants Camp. O, Impregnable Void Camp. O, My Prudent Parsimony Camp Camp. O, Herr of My Demotion Camp. O, for You Who Are Not the ONE Camp. And for you, Who Never Knew Me Camp. And, For You Who Cannot Come Undone Camp. O, *For You* Whom I've Built up Only to be Let Down Camp. *O, this is for you.*

CUNTSTRUCK

O, this is for you & you & you & you & you.

This is for you.

<<YOU are not just a character here.>>

                                              a one a one a one
                                    a one a one a one a one anew

.

CUNTSTRUCK

Herr Collarstays& Darts—*Ein Bisschen Phantasie Bitte!*

It's all about form—YES!

My Intractable Ruler, My Master of Conflation, O Herr Contraré!

Will you inform me?

When you finally realize you are not just a linebreak, an enjambment, an off-rhyme, a false alliterative aim?

CUNTSTRUCK

Or, must you merely maim me?
Go ahead then, MAIM.

I am not afraid.

Imprint me then, go ahead IMPRINT me.
Imprint me again then Silly
& Imprint me here again.

O, my Darling New Self-Abandonment!

I came to you in Staves —
I came to you Undone.

You came to me
in the Oceanic
Cliff-held flesh-held
bottle-capped waves —

CUNTSTRUCK

CADDISH

A FLAW A FLAW A FLAW

A choke-hold of exculpated Want
Latent Deeds. Harkened me forward

Wet streets —   sheeted knots
Untoward   Lacklove comparisons–

I knew it was through.   Courted
Ambivalence. Not interesting — Really,
No, merely replicated fuzzy frontiers —
illustrated weak character-lines.   Only.

               She did not.

WANT.

A FLAW A FLAW A FLAW

of laws OFF Relational ineptitudes,
false treatises.   Saveloy Contexts.

Crudenesses.

OFF easements & decorative battlements
off false adornments.

Seared words forespoke
Her Seaward wants.

SEAWORDS   fore-spake her

      Reduced
Reduced   Reduced

A FLAW A FLAW A FLAW

Once upon a Caddish night
The city showed itself
In trick light
Swelled

Brief Visual Reduction:

    VRAOUM!

du   du   du...

Detail me:

    du   du   du!

A FLAW A FLAW A FLAW

Language taught me unto myself twice.

Continues to upbraid me. Has never treated me right.

Bundles me up in prepositions—tells me to take speakers at their word.

Imperative designs! Uppercases my existence again and again.

La requalification de l'image.

        TEXTE

COMME
        LANGUE.

    LANGUE!

A FLAW A FLAW A FLAW

I came to on the isle of LANGUE—came again then—
Left bare.

                UTTERLY LONE,

do   do   do

Lettrage me!
        do   do   do
Rage me for
Wards
Word off
contempt

Undress text
here—

A FLAW A FLAW A FLAW

What is text really?

A flaw?

Chanced sole adrogynous.

I am not very good. I admit.

I abandon text again and again.

I only use it for my own advantage.

       Toot Allure!

Overtly estimated inordinate fears,
Repeat capricious ribaldry daily!

       à tout à l'heure!

A FLAW A FLAW A FLAW

Feats, (co)occurences

Typography as type
                  FATE
As final topography.
                  Offlaws.
Promulgation.

Wild distillations!
Disingenious Currencies.

Vraiment!!

A FLAW A FLAW A FLAW

Du lange,

Lies.

Nicht mehr! *Schau mal!*

Einführung:

BEGET BEGET BEGET
                              me

A(p)parent less by Capitalistic multitudes

& PHONIES who taunt Catcher in the Rye
As a human reaction manual….

We must boycott vapidity!
We must boycott false friends.
We must boykott those who are not courageous.
Who can not…   Who are not…

A FLAW A FLAW A FLAW

A CAD A CAD A CAD !

a flaw   a flaw   a flaw...

ISH!

A FLAW A FLAW A FLAW

THE, WE BOYCOTT AN ENTIRE PAGE OVERTURE HERE:

a flaw   a flaw   a flaw

>>fini<<

A FLAW A FLAW A FLAW

WE MUST EAT CAKE!
WE MUST EAT BEAUTY!
WE MUST EAT THE CADDISH NIGHT!

A FLAW A FLAW A FLAW

CAKEFEST FAKE TESTS HER BEST FURTHEREST COUNTESS OF OUR MESHED UP MURDERESS POR EST OUTVESTS TO GET HER NOW   A CAD A CAD A CAD TO GET HER ACCORDINGLY DEPRAVED SELECTMEN SNOTTY STYED TEXTED MINUTES VEX MY SELECTMAN *OH!* OUR TOYED VOWS OUR WANTON ECHOED NOWS DO NOT COWTOW ME DO NOT SOW MY RIVER WANTS   DO NOT SOIL MY WRESTED CITIFIED   MINUTEMEN   FALSEHOODS OR LONG FORGOTTEN MUTED CHILDHOOD TUTUS   *OH!* TUT TUT TUT MOVE ME ALONG AMONG MY OVUM TOTS SNOWY   WINTERED   ONYX   WONTING AND INTENSE SMUTTY DARLING DREAMS TUX TUX TUX NUTTY WOSTED VESSEL WANTS SETTLE SETTLE SETTLE ME NOW THEN MY WAXED PARRAFIN CONQUESTS

A FLAW A FLAW A FLAW

Poorest por est
                Forests wicked ache wants
Wicked wicked
      Dissonant wants.
Edging Old Sea.

Mental echo off Sirens calls

Masted

Masted Ulysses —

O, Master me Odysseus!

A FLAW A FLAW A FLAW

We die fighting.
We die hiding behind
our own wild disillusionments,

Ready to be Reborn.

A FLAW A FLAW A FLAW

Allowing the Codex

      VISERAL
VISUAL
        REAL

of Lexiconic
cut words
       cute words
             cuttingwards

finding other means to
undress the text here

which fools me
which fondles me

Wickedly

                    A PRIORI

TRIUMPH OF LOVE

*for Nadezhda Tolokonnikova, Maria Alyokhina,
and Yekaterina Samutsevich*

A FEMinist RIOT ManifestO
OR,- A PUSSY PRAYER
IN AN AGE OF DARKNESS

Because we all have a pussy riot inside of us.
Because we all have a pussy riot inside of us. SIR,-
sir sir sir sir sir sir sir sir sir
sir sir sir sir sir sir sir sir sir

OCCUPY
WAXED LIGHTS
Lorgnettes BRILLIANT LUNATICS!
Beautiful Idiots! We garnish charms.

As the feminist movement is DISPARATE
Good lace lattice-networking heliocentrists

Because we all have a pussy riot inside of us.
Because we all have a pussy riot inside of us. SIR,-
sir sir sir sir sir sir sir sir sir
sir sir sir sir sir sir sir sir sir
TRIUMPH OF LOVE

~~GOD~~LACED,-
This isn't about Legitimate Rape
But it is about Shutting that whole thing down…

Operating in darkness. Etched wrists of VERSO.
Your system politic is our system too. System POLITIC
as de-systemization of <u>SELF</u>
We must break down the self in order to break open the self
in order to radicalize thyself—and suffer greatly to publish
such SELF intention. In order to LOVE others we must
love Ourselves. Must tamp down wanton distraction & beckon
rEVOLution! Break out into the streets—break down the picturesque
OCCUPY
YOURSELF

Because we all have a pussy riot inside of us.
Because we all have a pussy riot inside of us. SIR,-
sir sir sir sir sir sir sir sir sir
sir sir sir sir sir sir sir sir sir

Sir our Aching girlhood wants HERSELF.
Masquerading WANTS herself tributaries in time in time
in time… winding round and round as ONE must
simply represent an other or two perhaps WANTS
then those two represent another four and so on. The children
will be with their mothers.

The children WILL be with their mothers.

Let us all represent each other representing our selves
SELF toward the greatest possible self in
repeat in repeat in repeat…ONWARDS

Because we all have a pussy riot inside of us.
Because we all have a pussy riot inside of us.
sir sir sir sir sir sir sir sir sir SIR,-
sir sir sir sir sir sir sir sir sir
TRIUMPH OF LOVE

GODSPEED,-

IN THE END

Susana Gardner is the author of *HERSO An Heirship in Waves* (Black Radish, 2011) and *[lapsed insel weary]* (The Tangent Press, 2008). Her poetry has appeared in many online and print publications including Cannibal, Jacket Magazine, How2, Puerto Del Sol, and Cambridge Literary Review among others. Her work has also been featured in several anthologies, including KINDERGARDE: AVANT-GARDE POEMS, PLAYS, STORIES, AND SONGS FOR CHILDREN, Black Radish Books, "131.839 slog meth bilum" (131.839 keystrokes with spaces), NTAMO, Finland and NOT FOR MOTHERS ONLY, a collection of poetry by women from Fence Books, USA. She lives in Zürich, Switzerland, where she also edits and curates the online poetics journal and experimental kollektiv press, DUSIE.

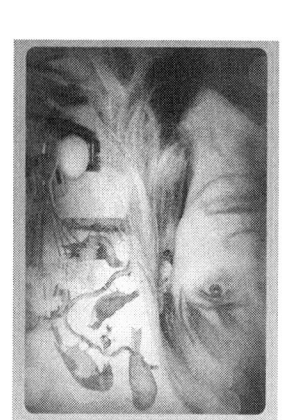